Needle Crafts 4

PATCHWORK

SEARCH PRESS
Tunbridge Wells

INTRODUCTION

Patchwork is a form of needlework in which fragments of cloth are joined edge to edge by stitching, or applied to a background of material. It is thought to be of peasant origin because of its economical use of scraps of costly or unobtainable cloth.

It has been suggested that patchwork was practised in the Middle and Far East long before the birth of Christ, but there are no more than passing references to it in Britain before the enthusiastic seventeenth-century revival of interest in the craft. The most productive period was approximately 1750-1850. Many patterns used in the North of England and in America were identical, so we may assume that early settlers in North America took the same patterns with them. The patchworkers of that period were very ingenious and planned and cut carefully to make the best use of their materials. They brought colour and pattern into largely sombre homes. Curtains, bed-covers, cushions and smaller articles were made of patchwork. The most popular shapes were squares, triangles, diamonds and rectangles which could be made by folding and cutting the material. Templates were not common until the mid-nineteenth century.

We are now experiencing another patchwork revival, again because it is economical and because results are attractive but also because hand-sewing the patches is restful. The finished work can be simple or complex. Patchwork can also be sewn more quickly by machine. Whichever method is used, the design is most important; time has to be spent on planning shapes, colours and layout.

This booklet offers instructions for patchwork by a number of methods. It does not however extend to dressmaking and other making-up techniques which are beyond its scope.

Pincushion. Hexagons in cottons, made into the traditional flower shape *(by Bridget Ingram)*.

Imitation suede bag. The suede was machined in strips from the back, then top machined on the front. The bag has a denim flap and strap, and is lined in vilene *(by Brenda Showler)*.

Pattern 1. Patterns using hexagons, half-hexagons, pentagons and diamonds drawn on isometric graph paper.

4

TOOLS AND MATERIALS

Templates

These are the master shapes from which the paper patterns are cut. They must be absolutely accurate. The size of the template is given as the length of one of the sides, whatever the shape may be. Most of the geometrical shapes in different sizes are produced commercially and can be bought in department stores or craft or needlework shops *(Fig. 1)*. They are made of thin metal and are usually sold together with a plastic 'window' template from which the fabric is cut *(Fig. 2)*. The window template is useful as the pattern on the fabric can be seen through it *(Fig. 3)*. Home-made templates can be made from card but they do not last very long.

Previous page:

Cotton cushion. A traditional design in floral patterned cottons in shades of brown and cream *(by Anne West)*.

Fig. 1. Some of the geometrical templates which can be used for patchwork.

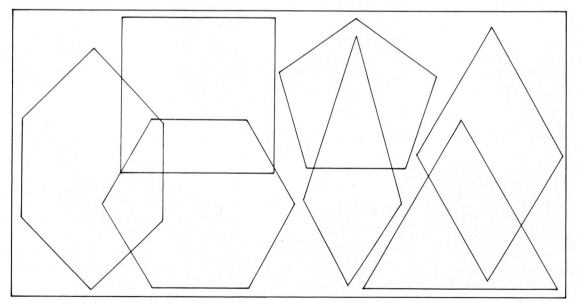

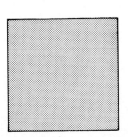

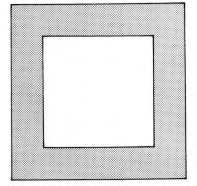

Fig. 2. A solid and a window template.

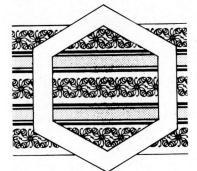

Fig. 3. A window template laid on the fabric to show the effect of the finished patch.

They can also be cut from thin metal or plastic, but as the shapes must be so accurate it is probably better to cut only large sizes and simple shapes at home.

Paper

The paper patches should be cut from paper or thin card stiff enough for the edge to be felt through the fold of the fabric. Magazine covers, Christmas cards, company reports or top quality writing paper are appropriate to different fabrics. Larger patches often need stiffer paper than smaller ones, however it must not be so stiff that it will not fold with the fabric as the work proceeds.

Fabrics

The best fabrics to use have a firm weave, are not too thick and crease well. Cotton is used most often and is probably the most satisfactory. You can also use linen, silk, wool, cotton-and-wool mixtures, corduroy and velvet. Man-made fabrics, except the stretch ones, are not so satisfactory as they can pucker and fray too much. Washable fabrics should be washed before being made into patches as some will shrink more than others, which will cause parts of the finished work to pucker. You can make very small patches only from the finer fabrics whereas the thicker fabrics will be easier to handle when covering larger shapes.

You must keep the same weight and type of fabric throughout the piece of work. If two patches of different weights are sewn together the heavier one will cause the finer one to tear, and it will be impossible to keep the patches the same size as the one covered with the finer fabric will be slightly smaller.

A fabric that is difficult to use for covering paper patches, such as leather, can be applied to a background without turnings.

Needles

Use fine needles. Size 9 and 10 are the best. For accurate sewing use a thimble.

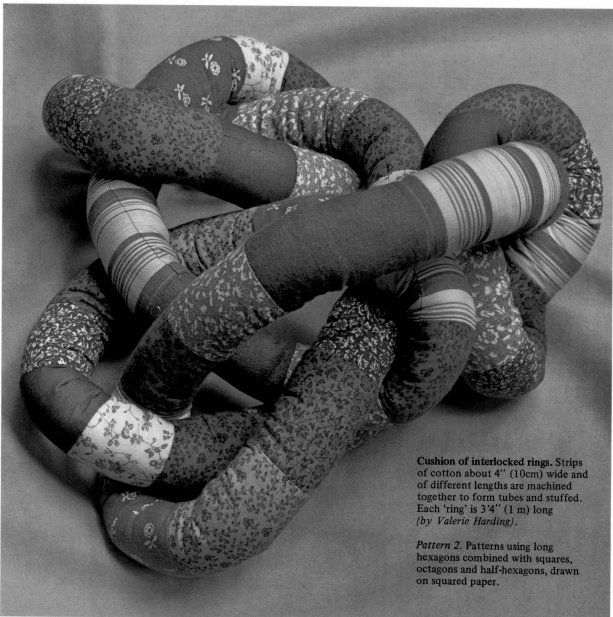

Cushion of interlocked rings. Strips of cotton about 4″ (10cm) wide and of different lengths are machined together to form tubes and stuffed. Each 'ring' is 3′4″ (1 m) long *(by Valerie Harding)*.

Pattern 2. Patterns using long hexagons combined with squares, octagons and half-hexagons, drawn on squared paper.

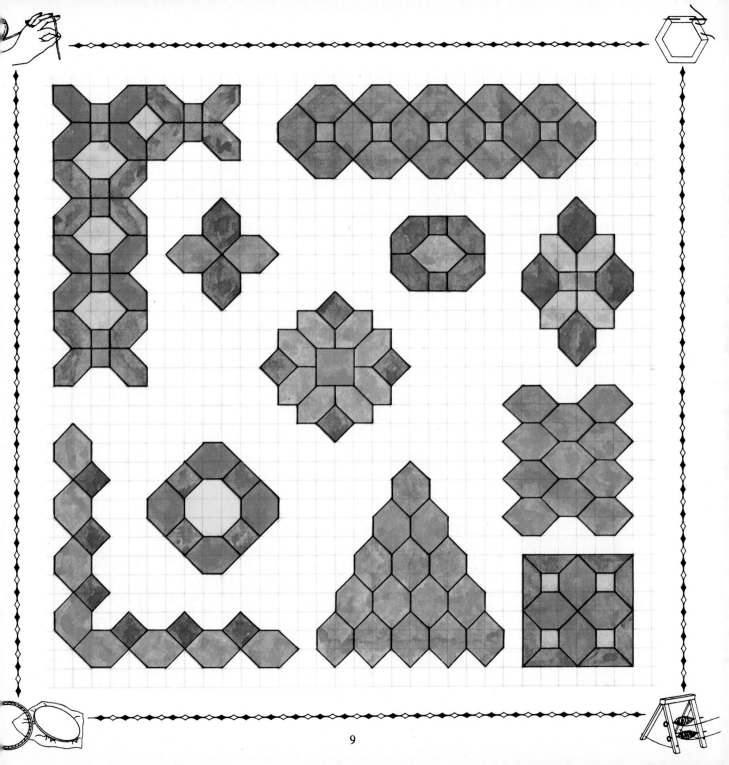

Scissors

You need paper scissors to cut the paper patches, and sharp medium-size scissors for the fabric.

Pins

Pins should be fine so that they do not mark the fabric; 'lills' or 'lillikins' are short and do not get in the way.

Thread

Use fine sewing thread; cotton thread will sew most fabrics. Try to match the colour of the thread to the fabric so that it shows less. If you are sewing a dark patch to a light one, use a dark thread.

Board

It is a good idea to have an insulating board or one made of thick card or cork, on which to pin the patches when planning the design. Pin the completed patches in place too so that you don't mix them up.

PATTERNS AND PATCHES

Paper patterns

You must cut paper patterns very accurately and there are two ways of doing this. One is to hold a piece of paper and a template together very firmly with the left hand so that they don't slip, and then to cut the paper with the blades of the scissors pressed up against the side of the template *(Fig. 4)*. Try to make only one cut for each side of the template. You can cut two paper patterns at once but no more. The second method is to cut the patterns on a board using a craft knife pressed against the side of the template.

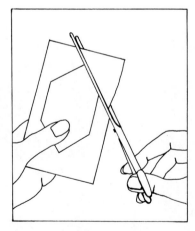

Fig. 4. How to cut paper or card patterns.

Do not draw round a template onto paper and then cut it out; the results will never be accurate. When enough patterns are cut out pin them to your board in the design you have planned and mark the direction of the grain on each one.

Fabric patches

For a first piece of work, use a fine firm cotton with a one-way pattern or a stripe that follows the direction of the grain, which is often difficult to see. The grain of every single patch in a single piece of work should lie in the same direction. That will make the work crisper and flatter, and it will wear better. Disregard this rule if the pattern of the fabric suggests otherwise, for example when stripes radiate out from a central point in the design.

Use the window template to cut the fabric patch as it allows adequate turnings and shows what the finished patch will look like. Hold the template and fabric firmly together and cut around the edges close to the template. You can also draw round the templates with a dressmaker's pencil.

Cut enough patches for a small section of your design and pin them to the board over the paper patterns, matching the grain marks.

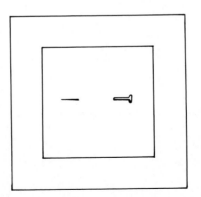
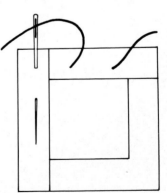

Fig. 5. The paper pattern is pinned to the wrong side of the fabric patch, making sure that the grain of the fabric is in the right direction.

Fig. 6. How to make a square patch.

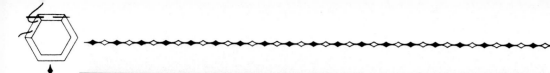

Tablecloth. Worked in various soft cottons, in 1″ (25mm) hexagons *(by Brenda Showler)*.

METHOD I – BASIC

Making the patches

The most usual way of making patches is as follows: lay the paper pattern in the centre of the fabric patch with the fabric the wrong side up. Pin the two together through the centre *(Fig. 5)*. Fold one edge of fabric over the paper and take a large stitch through all three layers (if the fabric is liable to mark, tack through the turning and paper only). Fold the second side of fabric over the paper and take a stitch through the fold, then another stitch through the centre of the side *(Fig. 6)*. With very small patches one stitch will do instead of two. Continue round all the sides, taking an extra stitch in the first side, and leave a short length of thread hanging free. The beginning of the thread can be knotted if you wish but if you make a large piece of work it will be much easier to take the tacking threads out at the end if there are no knots. The papers are left in the work until it is finished to keep it crisp and fresh.

The paper pattern can be replaced with one of vilene, felt, thin foam or some other material, depending on the result you want. These are quite difficult to handle and are best forgotten until some experience is gained with the paper patterns. Patterns of felt and vilene are left in when the work is finished to add body.

Sewing the patches

Patches are usually joined together by holding two patches together with the right sides of the fabric facing each other and the papers on the outside, and oversewing along the edge *(Fig. 7)*. Start the sewing about ¼″ (6mm) in from the corner, work back to the corner, then sew forwards to the next corner. Finish off by working back again for ¼″ (6mm). Make neat stitches, taking only a small amount of fabric each time and not sewing through the paper. With fine fabrics, sixteen stitches to 1″ (25mm) will

Fig. 7. Oversewing the patches together.

be about right. When the seam is finished and the patches are opened out the stitches will show on the right side and therefore must be even. You can sometimes seam together several patches with the same thread.

The other method of sewing patchwork is to stab-stitch the patches to a backing fabric, usually of cotton, which has been stretched on an embroidery frame. Bring the needle up through the background next to the edge of the patch and down through the patch and backing together. If the patch is made of a fabric that will fray then a small hem should be turned under before stitching it.

Machine-sewn patches

You can sew large patches by machine using a plain seam. There is no need to cut paper patterns; the fabric patches should have the outline of the template drawn on them and then be cut out leaving a seam allowance. Place two patches together with the right sides of the fabric facing each other and carefully match the drawn edges. Sew with a fairly short stitch, reversing at the beginning and end of the seam to secure the threads. Press the seams open.

Swing-stitch patches

Patches made of stiff leather or PVC can be cut leaving no seam allowance, placed edge to edge with corners matching, and swing-stitched on the right side.

Finer fabrics, or those which fray, should be backed with iron-on vilene before the swing-stitching, also on the right side. When using vilene start at one edge, place a row of patches in position and iron them so that they are firmly held. Do not allow the iron to go over the edge of the fabric or the base will become sticky. A second row is then put in place and ironed. Continue until a large area is covered with patches and then stitch them.

Pattern 3. Patterns using squares. Some of the squares have been divided in half to make triangles. They can also be divided to make smaller squares, rectangles or smaller triangles.

Overleaf:

Quilt. Different size stars are applied to a background worked in hexagons of white textured fabrics *(by Ann Dyer)*.

Hammock. Made of tubular strips of patchwork sewn by machine and stuffed, woven through string *(by Valerie Harding)*.

Method II – Log Cabin

This is quite different from the method already described and is built up using strips of fabric sewn onto a backing, working outwards from a central square. There are two possibilities:

Technique 1

To make log cabin patchwork, cut a square of calico or cotton about 6″ (15cm) square. This size will be right for cushions or bags, and for larger articles the square should be 12″ or 14″ (30cm or 35cm). Rule and number a template of card which is used for cutting the fabric strips *(Fig. 8)*. Then rule or fold diagonal lines on the calico square to find the centre and tack a 1¼″ (31mm) square of fabric to it *(Fig. 9)*. Cut a number of strips of fabric, each 1″ (25mm) wide and in varying lengths according to the template. It is usual to cut two pale and two dark strips of each length. Lay the shortest strip on the backing fabric with the right side down and the edge matching the edge of the tacked square. Stitch through all three layers, fold the strip back and press it. The second strip is sewn opposite the first *(Fig. 10)*, and then the two side strips.

Technique 2

Follow the first technique except that the strips are cut out double the width, folded along the length and pressed. The double strip is sewn to the backing fabric along the raw edges, leaving the fold free. This method makes a rather heavier form of patchwork.

When a number of squares have been made they are back-stitched together, or machine stitched, and the seams pressed open.

The pattern of log cabin depends on the placing of the pale and dark strips and the way the squares are sewn together *(Fig. 11)*.

Fig. 8. The card template for log cabin patchwork. Add ¼″ (6mm) seam allowance to all sides when cutting the fabric strips.

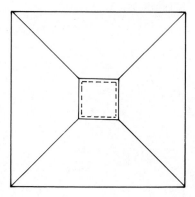

Fig. 9. The small fabric square is stitched to the backing square.

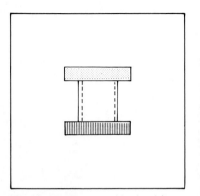

Fig. 10. The first two sides in place, sewn and folded back.

Fig. 11. The finished square, showing how one half is darker than the other in order to make the final patterns.

Pomander. Pentagons of lawn and lace, trimmed with pearl beads and ribbon, and stuffed with pot-pourri. The use of lace leaves openings for the fragrance of the pot-pourri to come through *(by Brenda Showler)*.

Log cabin cushion. Four squares of log cabin patchwork are fitted together to make this cushion *(by Val Tulloch)*.

METHOD III – STRIP PATCHWORK

An extension of log cabin patchwork is when strips of fabric are sewn to lengths of calico which are eventually sewn together to make various patterns. Long strips can also be seamed on the machine and then cut and rejoined.

METHOD IV – FOLDED SQUARES

2″ (50mm) squares of fabric can be folded to make a border of triangles *(Fig. 12)*. Each fold should be pressed before the next fold is made, and the raw edges of the triangles are enclosed in a seam. If ribbon is used instead of fabric the first fold is omitted.

METHOD V – PILLOW PATCHWORK

A method of sewing patches together and stuffing and lining them at the same time is called pillow patchwork. Two equal squares of fabric are cut and seamed together on three sides, with the right sides of the fabric on the inside. Trim the corners and turn inside out. Stuff the pillow with wadding (not cotton wool, which goes lumpy), turn in the edges of the opening and tack them together. Slip stitch the edges together. When a number of pillows have been made they are joined by oversewing or faggoting. This method can be used with triangles, hexagons or other shapes that fit together.

Fig. 12. Squares of fabric folded to make triangles for use as an edging.

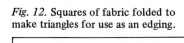

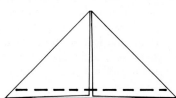

PLANNING THE DESIGN

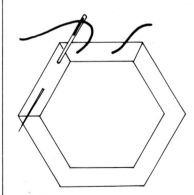

Waistcoat. An example of random patchwork, made into a waistcoat, in shades of blue and cream *(by Jane Lemon)*.

Colour and tone

These are very important in patchwork, with tone (which means how light or dark the colour is) being the most important. A patch that is the wrong colour is not nearly so noticeable as one that is too light or too dark. The importance of tone is shown by the three-dimensional effects obtained when dark, medium and light patches are sewn together in various ways.

Closely related colours make a pleasant muted scheme whereas contrasting colours are lively. For a first piece of work you can choose three related colours, such as blue, green and turquoise, with one of the colours fairly dark and one fairly pale. If the tones are too alike the pattern will be lost. Try to vary the proportions of the three colours and do not use equal quantities of any of them.

Collect as many fabrics as you can so that you always have a piece of the right colour or pattern for your design.

Geometrical patterns

A vast range of patterns can be made using bought templates in geometrical shapes. It is almost impossible for two people to produce the same design, even if they use the same shapes and fabrics.

The easiest shape to make in patchwork is the hexagon *(Fig. 13)*, but the long hexagon has more possibilities for pattern-making and combines well with other shapes. The square is extremely useful and can be sub-divided into triangles *(Fig. 14)*, rectangles, strips, and many more. The diamond is rather difficult to make because of the sharp point and is best left until more experience is gained.

Fig. 13. Making a hexagonal patch.

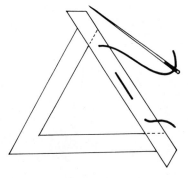

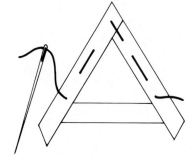

Fig. 14. Making a triangular or diamond-shaped patch.

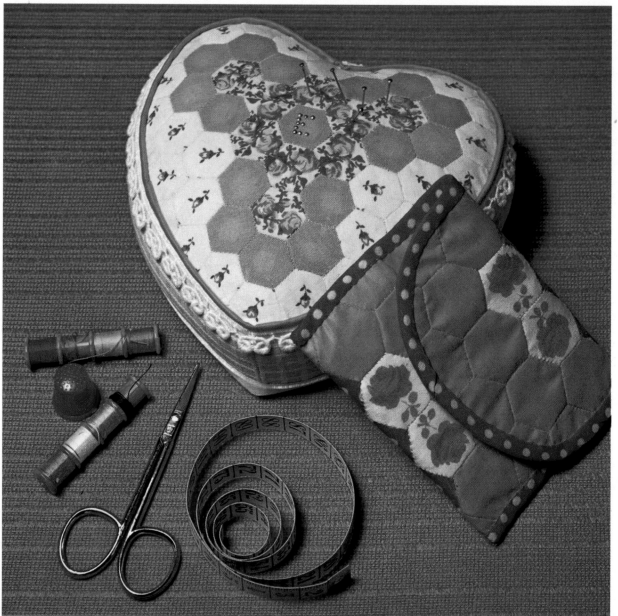

Heart shaped pincushion. Made in cottons with a ³⁄₈'' (10mm) hexagon, stuffed with kapok, and mounted on a cardboard base *(by Brenda Showler)*.

Needlecase. Worked in cotton in hexagons and diamonds, with a Velcro fastening *(by Brenda Showler)*.

Pattern 4. Interlaced octagon pattern. The shapes have been put together using the basic shapes — triangles, squares and octagons — shown at the top left corner of the illustration.

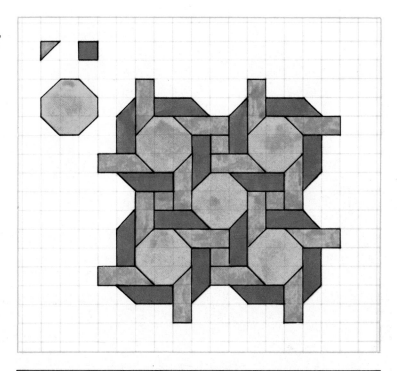

Geometrical shapes can be put together in long strips and then sewn together along the length. One strip could be of small squares, the next of triangles, the next of larger squares, and so on. This could be built up to make a complete cushion cover, skirt, or window blind. For a bed-cover, it would probably be more satisfactory to work outwards from a central square or rectangle.

Try to mix different shapes in your design to add variety. Many pieces of work can have a border around them or along one edge. The border colours can be paler or darker than the main part of the design, and the shapes can be larger or altogether different.

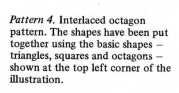

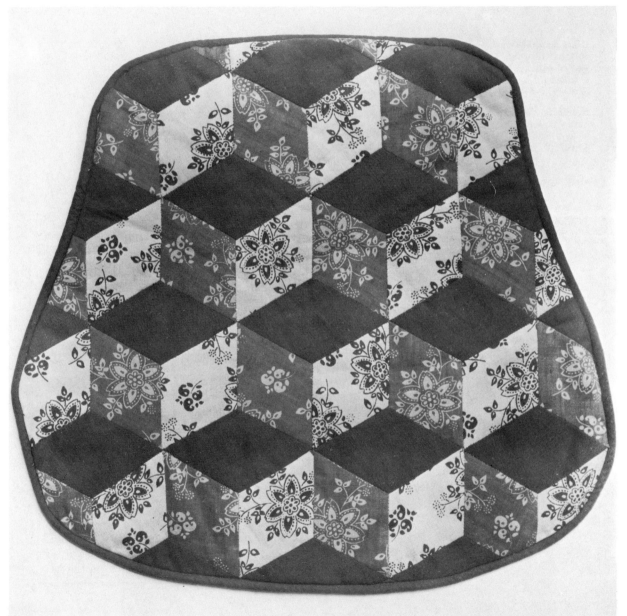

Cushion pad. Made of flowered and plain cottons, designed to fit a cane-seated chair. Padded with terylene wadding. 2″(5cm) diamond templates were used *(by Frances Collins)*.

Corners

These need careful planning. Some patterns will not turn a corner successfully, and the space must be filled with a plain shape such as a square, or a sub-divided square.

Stripes

Striped fabrics have immense possibilities in patchwork and a single piece of striped fabric can, with careful cutting and planning, be used to make a complete article. Sometimes a plain fabric can be combined with the striped one to emphasize the pattern.

Squared paper

An arithmetic book is useful for planning the designs and the colours can be filled in with felt pen. Isometric paper, which is divided into triangles instead of squares, is used for planning designs that include hexagons, triangles and diamonds.

Other sources of patterns

Mosaics, stained glass windows, tiled floors and other architectural details can all suggest patchwork patterns. Other crafts such as beadwork from Africa or North America, rugs, and woven cane chair seats all have patterns which might be adapted. Nature is always a rich source of inspiration and close-up photographs of many plants, shells, insects' wings or leaves reveal patterns that are not obvious at first.

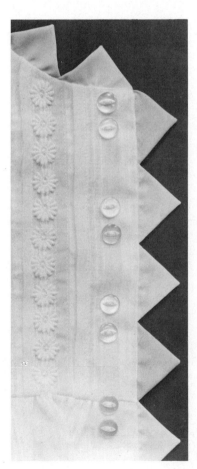

Ribbon edge. Ribbon used to make a folded edging, designed for a house-coat *(by Valerie Harding)*.

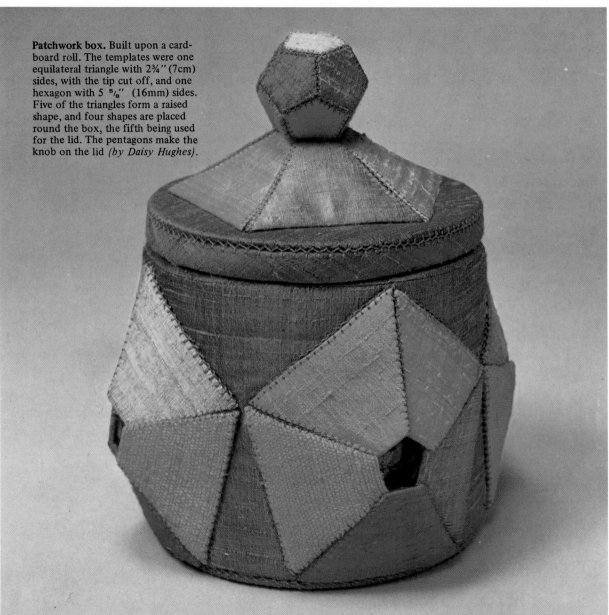

Patchwork box. Built upon a cardboard roll. The templates were one equilateral triangle with 2¾″ (7cm) sides, with the tip cut off, and one hexagon with 5 ⅝″ (16mm) sides. Five of the triangles form a raised shape, and four shapes are placed round the box, the fifth being used for the lid. The pentagons make the knob on the lid *(by Daisy Hughes).*

Handbag. Log cabin patchwork, with an unusual combination of fabrics, snakeskin, and leather *(by Stephanie Wood).*

Floor cushion. Floral and plain cottons in dark blue and red *(by Sharon Richards).*

Finishing

Pressing

When the patches have all been sewn together, remove the tacking threads. Then press the work on the wrong side and carefully take out the papers. Sometimes they can be used again.

Lining

Most patchwork should be lined to add body and hide the raw edges, and sometimes interlined for warmth or if the patchwork is to be quilted. Terylene or Courtelle wadding or Domette in the UK are good for interlinings and will wash well.

Edges

The lining can be machined to the patchwork with the right sides inside, and then turned right side out.

The edges of the patchwork and lining can be tacked together and then bound with a strip of fabric.

Another method is to fold the edges of the patchwork and lining to the inside and then stitch through all the layers close to the edge, either by machine or with a running stitch.

Whatever method you use, choose it because it is appropriate to the article you are making.

ACKNOWLEDGMENTS

Edited by Kit Pyman

Text and drawings by Valerie Harding

Photographs by Search Press Studios

Text, illustrations, arrangement and typography copyright © Search Press Limited 1978

First published in Great Britain in 1978 by Search Press Limited, Wellwood, North Farm Road, Tunbridge Wells, Kent TN2 3DR

6 th Impression 1985, Reprinted 1986, 1988, 1990

ISBN 0 85532 411 2

Made and printed in Spain by A. G. Elkar, S. Coop. Autonomía, 71 - 48012-Bilbao - Spain

Frontispiece:
Satin cushion. In black, white, and striped satin; a traditional design in unusual fabric, to be used in a modern setting of black leather and chrome *(by Helen Clarke).*

Back cover:
Dog. Made in a variety of cottons, using a 1″ (25mm) template. Stuffed with one piece of thick foam plastic cut slightly larger to give a firm fit. The papers were removed before making up *(by Frances Collins).*

Pincushion. Made of striped cotton material, in a 'humbug' shape. Cushions can be made like this, joining striped material, and making the length just over twice the width. Seam up the top and two sides, then match the seams in the middle of the bottom and sew across *(by Valerie Harding).*

Pig. Worked like a patchwork ball in felt, the legs are rolled strips of felt, and the nose is three applied circles. The tail is stiffened with wire *(by Jill Pickup).*